OLD FILEY
REMEMBERED

Compiled by

MICHAEL FEARON

HUTTON PRESS
1994

Published by the Hutton Press Ltd.,
130 Canada Drive, Cherry Burton, Beverley,
East Yorkshire HU17 7SB

Printed and bound by

Clifford Ward (Bridlington) Ltd.,
55 West Street, Bridlington, East Yorkshire
YO15 3DZ

ISBN 1 872167 57 8

CONTENTS

ACKNOWLEDGEMENTS

It is a pleasure to express my appreciation of the kindness of members of Filey Town Council and of the Trustees of the Filey Museum in allowing me to reproduce many photographs from their extensive collections.

I am also most grateful to Claire Fearon for help in preparing the typescript.

Michael Fearon
Filey
September 1993

INTRODUCTION

Filey's name suggests that there has been a community here for about 1200 years. If that estimate is correct, it means that for a thousand years Filey was a small and rather remote farming and fishing village situated away from the road linking Bridlington and Scarborough. This community of a few hundred people lived on, or very close to, what is now Queen Street.

In the late 18th Century its natural potential as a quiet resort slowly became recognised and in the 1830s plans were prepared for the development of what was to become New Filey. In early Victorian days progress took place rapidly and by the late 1850s much of The Crescent had been built and the area in front laid out as pleasure gardens. In the following years the number of shops in the town centre grew rapidly as did the adjacent residential areas.

However, in spite of this rapid growth, the two communities of Old and New Filey retained for many years their separate and distinct identities; an indication of this is that well into this Century, Queen Street contained over twenty shops which supplied almost all of the needs of the residents of Old Filey. Though much changed in recent years, this ancient street still retains something of the atmosphere of the old town.

This collection of photographs has been assembled, and is presented, in the hope that it will give some indication of what Filey was like in late Victorian and Edwardian days and how it subsequently developed. Perhaps too, the reader will gain an impression of how earlier Filonians lived and worked and of the ways in which visitors, particularly in Edwardian times , relaxed while on holiday here.

An additional wish is that those who are unfamiliar with the town will be enabled to understand some of the reasons why both residents and regular visitors regard Filey with real affection and are genuinely grateful to those who, in previous days, contributed positively to the creation of Filey as we know it today.

Chapter One:

THE TOWN; THE CRESCENT AND THE CHURCHES.

The Town

Once development had begun, New Filey grew rapidly; between 1811 and 1881 the population quadrupled and the town centre as we know it today became established. Now, the number of shops is little different from what it was a hundred years ago but the range is much changed; there are now no grocers or provision merchants but there are several places where food is cooked to be eaten elsewhere; a concept unknown in Filey's earlier days.

Aerial views of Filey are always interesting and if the date is not known those familiar with the town will enjoy attempting to date the photograph.

This one was taken out-of-season as is confirmed by the trees, the quiet roads and the almost deserted beach. The Grange Avenue Estate is under construction, the Crescent Gardens Bandstand features prominently and Filey School has not been built. These pointers, and others, suggest the photograph was taken about 1947.

Notice also the space where is now the Community Centre and the Railway Goods Depot on the site of Silver Birches.

This aerial view of Filey in 1952 is not very different from one that might be taken today but there are some changes which you might like to look for.
(By courtesy of *Yorkshire Regional Newspapers*).

These splendid studies of Northcliffe in 1900 show what was Filey's grandest private house soon after its completion. Designed by the well-known architect, W. H. Brierley, for Miss Elinor Clark of Clark's Sewing Cottons and of the same family as Kenneth Clark, the art historian, the house takes full advantage of its superb site. The formal garden was, for Filey, a unique feature and the stonework, now almost a century old, remains in splendid condition.

Filey's main commercial thoroughfare is shown here as it appeared in the mid-1920s. Premises on the left include Albin's Tea and Dining Rooms; Weatherhogg and Smith, antique dealers; Herbert Plows, butcher; Cambridge & Brown, grocers; Robert Waller, tailor; John Otley, chemist. On the right-hand side are the shops of Robert Marriner, boots and shoes, and T. W. Fisher, toys and stationery.

This view of John Street illustrates the premises of businesses whose names will be recalled by older Filonians; they include Harry S. Brigham, poulterer; H. C. Reed, clothiers; Fleetwood Hinchliffe, jeweller and antique dealer; A. E. Bulley, watch-maker; J. P. Rymer, decorator; F. Cappleman, ladies outfitters. Facing the street are the Co-operative Stores.
The nun in the right foreground is presumably returning to the Convent of the Sacred Heart (now the Town Hall).

The early confidence demonstrated by many in the growing commercial importance of New Filey is confirmed by the splendid edifice of the York City and County Bank at the corner of Murray Street and West Avenue in Edwardian days. The first shop in Murray Street is Hardwick's Boot Stores followed by the grocer's shop of Richard Scotter. He was regarded with affection and respect by many hard-pressed fishermen's wives for his willingness to extend credit during long winters of poor fishing.

At first glance it is hard to recognise this late Edwardian view as being one of central Filey.
It is, in fact, Station Avenue looking across to West Avenue.

South Crescent Villa was built in the 1850s and remained a private residence for many years. Shown here about 1910, it was then the home of Madge (later Dame Madge) Kendal, the well-known Shakespearean actress and her actor-manager husband, Kendal Grimston. It is now the popular White Lodge Hotel.

The fine proportions of Ravine Hall are evident in this late Victorian view. Built in the 1830s it was splendidly situated in the small estate we now know as the Glen Gardens.

In the late 1880s the house and estate were purchased by Edwin Martin, a Huddersfield mill-owner; the adjacent gill thus became known as Martin's Ravine. In later years it was a hotel and during World War II it was requisitioned by the military. This latter period began its decline which ended in its demolition in the 1960s. The Park Restaurant now occupies the site.

This attractive water-colour shows Ravine Hall as it was as a hotel in the 1930s.

11

The Museum in Queen Street is not Filey's first. As the post-card shows, there was a museum in 'The Cottage', a house between Queen Street and Mitford Street overlooking the sea. Open for a short period about 1910, little is now known about it but clearly it possessed some interesting displays of early pottery.

Fortunately, serious fires have been rare in peace-time Filey. The three most serious, perhaps, being that of a furniture store, shops and stables behind No. 7 The Crescent in October 1890, the Wesleyan Methodist Church and the Victoria Hall in Murray Street in 1918. The Church was re-opened in 1823.
This fire, which clearly could have been more serious, was at 10 John Street on 8th January 1920.

Much of Filey's plumbing from the early part of the
Century onwards was carried out by G. H. Cambridge
Ltd. The firm was also responsible for much gas-fitting as
the window display indicates. The premises stood in
Mitford Street opposite to where is now the Fire Station;
they have been considerably altered.

The main structure of the mill on Muston Road still
remains as a prominent feature.
This turn-of-the-Century study shows what marvels of
engineering such devices were.

This mid-Edwardian era view shows the terrace of houses then known as Ravine Bank but which is now identified as 89-103 West Avenue. The ornate iron railings and gates were an important architectural feature; no doubt they would be taken for scrap as a contribution to the war effort in the early 1940s.

The milk-cart with its large churn is a reminder of how milk was then delivered; the occupant has been identified as Joe Colley.

The sheer bulk of the 'Old Royal', (the Royal Hotel), dominates Belle Vue Street in this early 1920s view. Built in the 1850s, it was not a success as a hotel and was soon sub-divided into individual residences and businesses. It was demolished about 1935.
At the corner of Belle Vue Street and West Avenue was the green-grocer's shop of Henry Walker, his market-garden was close to the Sea-dale railway crossing.

It may be surprising to learn that the photographer was standing at Filey's town centre when he captured, on film, this wintry scene about 1910.
This fine avenue of trees encloses Station Avenue; the Wesleyan Methodist Church is in the right foreground.

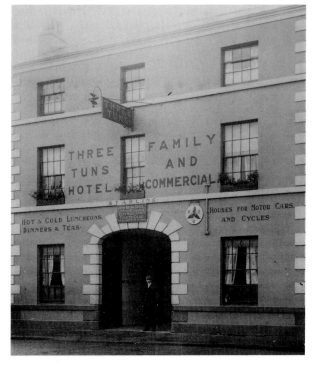

The coaching-inn origins of the Three Tuns Hotel are evident in this pre-World War One photograph. The licensee was John Brian Steel who may be the gentleman standing in the entrance. The circular emblem on the wall indicated that the hotel was a recommended hostelry for members of the C.T.C., the Cyclists' Touring Club.

As these photographs show, window and shop-front displays of the old-style family grocers were very carefully arranged and could often be considered works of art. Mr. and Mrs. G. E. Smithson at 83 Queen Street provided a vital service for residents of Old Filey as did the business of Samuel Towse for New Filey. This shop was situated at 1 Murray Street next to the entrance to Northcliffe and the figure in the entrance of the shop is almost certainly the owner-manager, Thomas Richard Towse. The business was later taken-over by the Co-operative Society.

Mitford Street (previously known simply as Back Street) formed the southern boundary of Old Filey. The name commemorates
Admiral Mitford of Hunmanby Hall who had considerable land and property in Filey.
The most prominent building to be seen is the Albert Hall, previously Bethesda Primitive Methodist Chapel
until replaced in 1870 by Ebenezer Chapel.
The building on the extreme right is the shop of John Harper, Corn Merchant.
It was, in 1811, Filey's first Wesleyan Methodist Chapel.
The photograph was taken at five minutes past eleven on Thursday, 8th September 1960 as part of a traffic survey
by Filey Urban District Council.

CLIFF HOUSE, FILEY.

When Cliff House was built in the early 1840s it would have had an uninterrupted sea-view. However, this was lost in 1851 when the terrace, 1-7 Crescent was erected. The blocking-up of several window spaces, presumably to avoid window-tax, must also have deprived the house of much natural light. Charlotte Brontë stayed with the Smith family, (who lived there for many years), in June 1849 following the death in Scarborough of her sister Anne. She stayed there again for a month in the early summer of 1852.

The house is now a popular shop and café.

CONVENT OF THE SACRED HEART, FILEY.

Members of the Roman Catholic order of nuns, the Sisters of Charity, came to Filey in 1904 and the following year, established as a high school for girls, the Convent of the Sacred Heart. It became an integral part of Filey's community and was much missed when it closed in 1969.

The building was taken over by Filey Urban District Council and is now the Town Hall; it remains structurally little changed. That part which is now the Concert Hall was originally the school gymnasium.

The Crescent

Few terraces of domestic buildings in the whole of England group so well together and, combine with that attribute an unrivalled outlook across pleasure-gardens to the sea. The Crescent is indeed an asset of which Filey is justly proud. When first built, all the properties with the exception of the Crescent Hotel, were private residencies or boarding-houses. Later amalgamations saw many converted to hotels and later still, to blocks of flats or, as in the case of the Hylands Hotel, a residential home.

It is fortunate that these conversions resulted in little change in external appearances and also that owners maintain their properties to commendably high standards.

This somewhat idealised lithograph of the Crescent in mid-Victorian days indicates a too great curvature to the gardens, resulting in a much wider road-width at the north end than is actually the case. The elegance of a 'select' resort is, however, well conveyed.

This scene represents what many think of as the elegance of Edwardian Filey. The year is about 1905 and the very formal attire suggests that the day is Sunday.

The shadows confirm that it is about mid-day in high summer so we can safely assume that the visitors are taking part in the traditional 'parade' through the Crescent Gardens following attendance at morning service.

19

This splendid late Victorian photograph of The Crescent surely indicates why many believe it to be
one of the finest terraces in England.
It is indeed a tribute to John Wilkes Unett, the Birmingham solicitor and co-founder of the Birmingham Society of Arts, to whose
design much of New Filey was built. He it was who, in 1835, insisted that pleasure-gardens should be an essential feature
of the whole concept.

It is regrettable that the name of this fine group of musicians is not known. They entertained visitors and residents throughout the 1905 Season while playing in the Crescent Gardens bandstand.

A turn-of-the-Century view of the Crescent Gardens with an early bandstand as its focal point. This bandstand (or music-stand as it was described in the Crescent Gardens Committee minutes) was later replaced by a colonnade and open lower-level dance area with central bandstand. In 1961 this area and bandstand were themselves replaced by the small concert hall known as the Sun Lounge.

FILEY BRIGG FROM CRESCENT GARDENS

The central feature of this 1930s view of the Crescent Gardens is the pay-box at the entrance; an admission charge was made for those who wished to stroll through the gardens and listen to the orchestra playing in the bandstand.

This excellent 1930s postcard (opposite page) of the Royal Crescent Hotel confirms what small changes have been effected in the outside appearance of the building in the last sixty years, although it ceased to be an hotel in 1960. There is however now no longer the side entrance shown in the photograph.

We can be grateful that this most imposing of Filey's buildings, occupying as it does, a key position in the centre of The Crescent, still retains much of the splendour it had when it possessed one of the finest of holiday addresses in the North of England.

A homely touch is given to the grand façade by the bathing costume drying at the second-floor corner window.

Because the local weekly paper, the *Filey Post*, (which was published from 1865 to 1918), included lists of visitors to the town, we know the names of many of those who stayed there during its 106 years as a leading hotel.

The brief excerpts from the Visitors' Lists show just a very few of the many thousands who enjoyed holidays there; the publication dates are 29 August 1872 and 9 July 1910. Also shown are some of those staying on the Crescent in July 1910. An interesting social comment is the number of maids, nurses and governesses appearing in the list.

List of Visitors.

Crescent Hotel.

Viscount and Lady Folkestone and suite
Nunappleton, Tadcaster
Lord Lascelles — Harewood House
Captain Brabazone — London
The Hon and Rev the Dean of Windsor
Windsor Castle
Herbert Fordham, Esq Mrs and fam
Odsey, Royston
Major-General Hutchinson — London
Mrs Hutchinson and family — London
Colonel Ford and Party
Hereford Gardens, Park lane, London
G W Alder Esq — Wakefield
William Peach Esq — Hornsey, London
Mrs Peach and fam — do
Charles Gould Esq — Inner Temple
Captain Gascoigne — Scots Fusileer Guards
Wm Greetham Esq — Stainsfield Hall, Lincolnshire
Thomas Greetham Esq — London
Thomas Barber Esq — Huddersfield
Samuel Shepherd Esq — London
— Laforne Esq — Denmark Hill, London
Mrs Laforne and fam — do
Charles Allison Esq — London
Mrs C Allison — do
Mrs George Blunt — do
— Farquhar Esq — London
Mrs Farquhar — do
Sam Hollins Esq — Astley Bridge, Bolton

LIST OF VISITORS.

ROYAL CRESCENT HOTEL.

Mrs Kemp, Manageress.

Their Royal Highnesses The Grand Duke and Duchess of Hesse, Suite and servants
The Hereditary Grand Duke George and Prince Ludwig
Her Royal Highness The Princess Louise of Battenberg and servants
The Duke of Abercorn, K.G
Baron F Massenbach — Darmstadt
The Baroness G Rotsmann
The Hon. Edith Winn — Nostell Priory, Wakefield
H E Harris, Esq — Hove
The Hon G W Winn and Mrs
Walton Hall, Wakefield
Sir Algernon F Firth, Bart and Lady — Halifax

THE CRESCENT.

2 Mrs Cunningham
Lord Bolton and Lady
Miss Powlet, governess and friend — Leyburn
3 Mrs Sowden
Mr Lockwood, Mrs, baby and nurse — York
4 Miss Smith
Mrs Forbes and maid — Gate Helmsley, York
Master Forbes and nurse — Stamford Bridge
H L Williamson, Mrs, baby and nurse
Headingley, Leeds
5 Mrs Colley
Misses Barker (3) — Sheffield
6 Mrs Cammish
Mrs Gawans, fam and nurse
Emley Woodhouse, Wakefield
7 Miss Perryman
Mr Willie R Heaven, Mrs, fam and nurses
Harrogate
Miss Freeman, and party — Manchester
12 Mrs Gibson
Col Starkey, Mrs and fam — London
14 Mrs Gardener
H J Morris, Esq, Mrs, fam and nurses
Ecclesthorpe Hall, Doncaster
Geo Hargraves, Esq, Mrs, fam, governess
and nurses — Hessle
C G Spencer, Esq, Mrs and fam — Bradford
R M Lees, Esq, Mrs and fam — Bradford
16 Mrs Barwick
Mr J Briggs, J.P., and Miss
Sandal Magna, Wakefie'd
G Briggs, Esq — Wakefield
Mr Moyley and Mrs — Nottingham
17 Mrs Haxby
Rev Merryweather, Mrs and Miss
St Philip's Vicarage, Sheffield
Mrs Blakeney
Mrs Sharman — Sheffield
18 Mrs Cammish
Mr Pickering and Mrs — Prescot, Lancashire
21 Mrs Flemming
Mr Forgan, Mrs and fam — Northwich
Mr C R Forgan, Mrs and fam — Northwich
Mrs Stanley and fam — Wath-on-Dearne
Mr Gamenon and Mrs — Hull
27 Mrs Hall
Mr Law, Mrs, children, and governess Rotherham
P H Shires, Esq, Mrs, fam and governess
Cheadle, Cheshire
28 Mrs Waggitt
Mr Jas Rhodes and Mrs — Rotherham
Rev C Bolam, Mrs, fam and nurse — Lincoln
Mr Parkin and Mrs — Sheffield
29 Mrs Bailey
Mrs Eccles, fam, and nurse Priors
Hardwick, Byfie'd
Mr P T Chadwick, Mrs, fam and nurse — Dewsbury
30 Mrs Johnson
Mr Anderson, Mrs, baby and nurse — Carlisle
Dr Godson, Mrs, Misses (3), and governess
Cheadle, Manchester
Mr Ned Godson and Mrs — India
Mrs Wetters — Cheadle

This mid-1950s view of the North and South Crescent Gardens confirms how great an asset they are to Filey as a resort. The central feature is the Crescent Gardens bandstand; it was replaced by the Sun Lounge in the early 1960s.

This lithograph of the Wesleyan (later Trinity Methodist) Chapel shows the building as originally designed. The main entrance and tower were somewhat changed before building commenced in the mid-1870s.

This stark photograph shows the Wesleyan Chapel soon after the disastrous fire in January 1918; the cause of the fire was never established.
Soon after the fire a re-building campaign began and on 7th March 1923 the chapel re-opened.

Churches

Filey's active church life is centred on the Anglican Churches of St. Oswald and St. John, the Roman Catholic Church of St. Mary, the Methodist Church and the Salvation Army Hall.

This small selection of photographs shows St. Oswald's, the Methodist Church before and after a serious fire, Ebenezer Chapel and, for its human interest, a Sunday School Treat.

The location for this Sunday School Treat of the Wesleyan Chapel about 1880 was Grange Farm, Muston Road.
The farm-house stood where is now the first entrance to the Wharfedale Estate.
Sunday School Treats were eagerly anticipated events and rewards for the pupils for regular attendance.
The children would race, play games and enjoy an open-air tea of sandwiches, cakes and fruit.
Having a photograph taken was an unusual event; perhaps this accounts for the somewhat serious countenances
of both young and old.

A question that is still unresolved is why, when Filey was a small village, did it merit such a large parish church. Generations of parishioners have also wondered, especially during spells of bad weather, why St. Oswald's was built at the side of Church Ravine distant from the community it served.

This late Victorian view illustrates well the church's cruciform design.

Ebenezer Chapel was a splendid example of Primitive Methodist architecture as this view indicates. It was built to the design of Joseph Wright who was a pupil of Cuthbert Brodrick and who was later to be responsible for many fine Methodist chapels. Known from its opening in 1870 as the Fisherman's Chapel, it witnessed many stirring occasions and the singing of a congregation of over seven hundred accompanied by the superb organ was, for any one present, a memorable experience. The Chapel closed in 1975 when the two Methodist causes were united.

Church Ravine

Filey is fortunate in having two natural boundaries; they are Martin's Ravine and Church Ravine. Both were probably created, (like several more in Filey Bay), as melt-water channels at the end of the last ice-age, about 12,000 years ago. For a period until 1889, Church Ravine formed part of the boundary between the North and East Ridings of Yorkshire.

We think of Church Ravine as being shaded by many mature trees; it was not always so as this print of about 1850 shows. Many of the trees were planted in the early 1870s when the stream was culverted, a road made and the whole Ravine landscaped by the recently formed Filey Local Board.
The stone bridge was damaged beyond repair by a flash flood following a storm in 1857.

One of the greatest changes to life in Filey during this century has been occasioned by the advent of the motor-car. This is indicated by comparing this view of Church Ravine in late summer about 1900 with the scene to be observed now, in the same place, and at the same time of year.
Clearly it was not then thought necessary to remove the trees in the centre of the picture even though they were growing almost in the road.

The Foreshore

The individuality of buildings on the Foreshore, where many different styles are represented, is in sharp contrast to the uniformity of the Crescent. However, to residents and visitors alike, both are equally acceptable and well complement each other.

Substantial buildings were erected on the Foreshore at times when the sea-defences would seem to have been inadequate, yet there is no indication that serious damage occurred at periods of high-tide and storm.

The construction of the sea-wall created spacious grounds which are well used during the holiday season, especially when the incoming tide has covered the sands.

This very early view of the Foreshore shows in the foreground the premises of local boat-builders. The detached house in the centre of the picture is Belvedere Villa; it was later demolished. The original Coastguard Station in Queen Street can be seen with its bad weather look-out. Also to be seen is the roadway which once led from Mitford Street to Queen Street.

The solid construction of bathing-machines is apparent from this view of the Crescent Hill slipway. These particular machines were hired-out by Herman Wright (the author's great-uncle) and would be horse-drawn to the water's-edge. Was it perhaps the costumes of the bathers which drew so many onlookers to the Promenade railings?

The urgent need in the late 1880s for major new sea-defence works is very evident from this study. Winter storms must have caused considerable anxiety to Foreshore residents.

This is one of Filey's rare, historic-event, photographs. The date is 24th April 1893 and Mrs. Edwin Martin of Ravine Hall is about to lay the foundation stone for the building of the sea-wall. The contractor, Mr. James Dickson of St. Alban's, stands at her right. Gathered for the great occasion is a splendid range of late-Victorian characters and even the school-boys appear to have been given permission to occupy any vantage point.

The mallet and trowel held by Mrs. Martin are in the possession of the Town Council. All credit is due to these Victorian builders, the wall has well withstood storm and tide for almost a century.

With what relief must residents have witnessed the commencement and completion of the sea-wall and Promenade. This photograph can be accurately dated to the early Summer of 1894; the official opening took place on 19th June, of that year and the carts in front of the cottages were used in the construction work.

The Donkeys, Filey

Donkeys and ponies wait at the foot of Crescent Hill to take children back to hotel or boarding-house after a tiring session on the beach.

The willingness of formally-dressed ladies to sit on the grass bank suggests that there were fewer dogs in Edwardian Filey. The performance they are watching so attentively is, of course, that of the Filey Pierrots, who are also providing a welcome diversion for the fishermen waiting to take visitors for a sail.
There is no record of Edward VII visiting Filey so no doubt the standing spectator is one of the many who adopted his dress and appearance.

The French Chateau influence, not seen anywhere else in Filey, is apparent in this photograph of an immaculate Ackworth Hotel.
The scaffolding around Deepdene shows it to be in the course of construction, confirming that
this Foreshore scene is of the early 1900s.
Even on holiday a certain formality of dress was clearly expected in Edwardian Filey
and almost no-one has ventured out without a hat.

In the Summer many Filey men would take a break from fishing to go 'spawing' — taking visitors for a row or sail around the Bay.
As this photograph shows, the Promenade bridge was a popular setting-off point.
The calmness of the sea indicates that a smooth trip for the passengers would be assured although the absence of wind would mean a tiring spell on the oars for the boat-crews.

This is one of the very few photographs of an activity which brightened cold Wintry days for many young and not-so-young Filonians. Sledging down Cargate Hill could be exhilarating, although if the surface became icy, negotiating the necessary turn on to Foreshore Road was a challenge not all participants could meet. Broken limbs sometimes resulted from an unintended descent of the grass bank.
Both Crescent Hill and Ravine Hill provided similar Winter sport.
After World War Two the increases in motor traffic and the gritting of roads brought sledging in Filey to an end.

Kingston Cottage, a substantial property with a prime position on Cargate Hill, was demolished about 1930; presumably the reason was in order to extend the gardens of Northcliffe.

STEPS TO THE BEACH
FILEY

ARQ

The artist, A. R. Quinton, has captured well the combination of Carr Naze, sea and sand in a frame of shrubs and trees which many find so attractive as they make their way to the Coble Landing.

Built about 1902, Deepdene was for over half-a-century one of Filey's largest private houses.
Subsequently it was converted into flats before eventually becoming dis-used.
The extensive site on the Foreshore was to have been re-developed in the late 1980s by the building of
a large block of flats but this was prevented by the decline in the housing market.

The Coble Landing

The Coble Landing on a fine Summer's day with its combination of life-boats, cobles and pleasure craft holds a ceaseless fascination for visitors to Filey. It has, of course, a very different appearance hours before a Wintry dawn as fishing-boats are being prepared for launching into the surf. However, both are fundamental aspects of this essential feature of Filey's life.

Filey has something of an out-of-season look in this late 19th Century view.

Fishing as an occupation has always been unusual in that much of the capital investment comes from the workers themselves. As this pre-World War I view shows, the monetary value of cobles, yawls, sails and fishing gear was considerable; when losses occurred because of stress of storm, a period of years might elapse before the damage could be made good.

These tranquil scenes of the Coble Landing and Bay convey something of the atmosphere of late Victorian days so many visitors found irresistible.

This rare coloured postcard, reproduced here in black and white, of the beach and Coble Landing evokes something of the atmosphere of local fishing at the end of the Edwardian era. The card was, in fact, posted one day after King Edward VII died.

Had the press photographer from the *Yorkshire Herald*, the celebrated painting 'The Boyhood of Raleigh' in mind when he composed this evocative study on the Coble Landing about 1930? The identity of the attentive listener is not known but the story-teller was a well-known Filey character, Mr. Healand Sayers.
(By courtesy of the *Yorkshire Gazette* and *Herald*).

Chapter Three:

THE BRIGG AND THE BEACH.

The Brigg

Bridlington's town crest incorporates three Bs whose symbolism is uncertain; Filey's three Bs are easy to identify; they are its Bay, Beach and Brigg. All these features contribute to the creation of a resort which many regard as being very special. The third of these natural assets provides shelter for vessels in the Bay and is also one of the finest places on the English coast for walking on sea-girt rocks.

This print shows Filey Spa as it was at the height of its popularity in mid-Victorian days. Its location was at the north side of Carr Naze above 'Black-hole'. Cliff erosion has now removed the whole site completely.
The Spa was centred upon a small spring which supplied water with supposedly curative properties. John Cole, in his 1828 *History of Filey*, recommended taking the water for dyspepsia, hypochondriasis, rheumatism and ailments of a scrophulous nature!

The rocks of Filey Brigg change only slowly with time having the solidity of their estimated age of 150 million years.
The glacial deposit clay of Carr Naze, laid down perhaps 15,000 years ago is much less durable and is much affected by ice, rain and wind.
A comparison between this view and a comparable one today will indicate how much change has taken place in 100 years.

That this view of the Brigg is almost 90 years old, confirmed by the dress of the ladies standing close to High Brigg and also the presence of the tea-hut; it was the first of several such establishments to occupy the site.

For many there is no finer way of being by the sea than by scrambling on Filey Brigg. Something of its grandeur is conveyed in this study which also shows Robert Maulson who, as the Brigg Attendant in pre-World War I days, assisted, for a small consideration, those adventurous enough to explore the Brigg's rocks and pools.

If the spray which forms a back-drop for the three Edwardian ladies is genuine they are displaying a remarkable nonchalance. However, perhaps it was added by the photographer to enable the group to be more clearly seen and to create a little drama.

Whatever may be the case, the stratified nature of the Brigg is shown to great effect in this view.

This Brigg café is a tribute to its builders who well overcame the problems associated with the location. Before World War Two it was a welcome sight to rock scramblers but it was demolished in October 1939 by a sea-mine exploding on impact after drifting on to the Brigg.

The Beach

It is almost certain that the gently-shelving beach of Filey Bay provided a point-of-entry for the Angles, Saxons and Vikings who came as raiders or colonisers in the centuries following the Roman occupation. In later years generations of Filey men launched their fishing boats from the sands. Now recognised as being one of the finest on the East Coast, the beach has been a major factor in the establishment of Filey as an important holiday resort.

The beach and Foreshore Road are shown here in the mid-1880s. The building at the extreme right is the original Lifeboat House which was replaced in 1892.

The old sea-wall which protected the Foreshore until replaced by the new Promenade is clearly shown in this 1880s scene. Downcliff, the large house in the centre of the photo, was built for and lived in by John Unett, the son of Birmingham solicitor John Wilkes Unett, the man mainly responsible for the planning and building of New Filey.

This panoramic view well illustrates the separate nature of Old and New Filey in late Victorian times. Two yawls are beached for the purpose of unloading fish and loading stores in preparation for the next trip which would probably be to the Dogger Bank, far out in the North Sea.
The primitive nature of the Coble Landing is perhaps surprising when bearing in mind that the Filey fishing-fleet then consisted of about 30 yawls, 15 large herring-cobles and 50 smaller boats.

This view of Foreshore Road can be reliably dated as 1893 as it shows the Promenade in its early stages of building. Completed the following year at a cost of about £12,000 its excellent design and construction resulted in an asset of which Filey is justly proud.

Donkeys have been an essential feature of the beach scene at Filey for well over 100 years. This group waits for business in the Summer of 1905.

The popularity of the 'Royal Filey Pierrots' is indicated by the sizeable crowd they have attracted to their performance on the beach in front of Martin's Barrier. The fashionable dress of the spectators suggests the period is Edwardian.
Two things that clearly change little with time are the fascination that pools of water have for children and the design of deck-chairs.

Prominent in this 1920s view of the beach are the beach-huts. They were the successors to the bathing-machines which had much larger wheels on which they could be drawn by horse to the water's-edge. A few years later they were themselves succeeded by the canvas beach-tents.

This delightful water's-edge scene in early Twentieth-Century Filey captures several of the familiar elements of the holiday resort; sailing-cobles, fishermen, fashionably-dressed visitors and the back-drop of Speeton cliffs.

The atmosphere of an Edwardian day is well captured here; even on the beach a degree of formality was expected as the jackets and caps of the boys indicate. Two bathing-machines wait close to the water's edge for holiday-makers keen to try a dip in the sea. The regularity of the Crescent roof-lines without the dormer-windows, introduced later, is apparent. The Crescent Hill terrace of houses has yet to be built and Swiss Cottage (next to Downcliff) is as originally constructed.

The calm sea and absence of sails suggest that the boatmen will have to row their passengers around the Bay. However, being fishermen they will be experienced oarsmen.
In Edwardian times, clearly, standards of dress could not be relaxed even for a boat-trip.

Children's Corner was the name by which this part of an early sea-wall, close to Crescent Hill, was known.
The entertainments available to these late Edwardian holiday-makers include performances by the Pierrots, a coconut shy, pony and donkey rides and the services of a photographer.

The striped beach-tents give an almost Eastern effect to Filey Beach in this mid-Edwardian (1906) view.

The number of boys and girls who have dammed and diverted the stream from Martin's Ravine on to the beach must now total many thousands. Here is just one young Edwardian engrossed in that particular activity.
The purpose of the groyne was to reduce the eroding effect of wave action on the cliff.

This between-the-wars view of beach and foreshore shows the rudimentary nature of the Coble-Landing sea-defences. The buildings on the Landing are boat-builders' workshops, the refreshment-rooms of Mr. Sidney Baker and the Lifeboat-House.

In late Victorian days, Edwin Martin, a Huddersfield mill-owner, purchased the Ravine Villa estate. The grounds now constitute the Glen Gardens. In order to prevent cliff erosion he arranged for the building of the wooden barrier which bore his name. It was popular with visitors but in January 1953 it was storm-damaged beyond repair and replaced in 1955 by the Royal Parade.

For residents of and visitors to Filey an impromptu and free eye-sight test would sometimes be carried out while standing in the Crescent Gardens. This was done by measuring the ease with which 'the submarine' could be seen on the rocks across the Bay.

It was a British submarine, number G.3, which broke loose while being towed to be broken up after World War One. It drifted ashore under Speeton Cliffs and remained visible there for several years. Much was subsequently taken for scrap but the massive batteries and other parts remain.

This view of the beach-tents belonging to the local firm of Burr and Fell typifies for many, pre- and early post-war Filey. They provided shelter from the occasional shower, a place in which to change and became veritable homes-from-home on long hot summer days. Spring tides, when the sea completely covered the beach, meant hard work for those whose job it was to move the tents, then dismantle them and store them on platforms built into the cliff.

The large number of holiday-makers on this one section of the Beach in the 1930s is remarkable, especially when bearing in mind that most would actually be staying in Filey itself in hotel, boarding-house or private home.

The Bridge, Arndale

The bridge crossing the stream at Arndale is seen here as it was until the 1960s. During World War Two the small valley was a place of danger because of the land-mines placed there as part of the coastal defences against invasion.

Primrose Valley. Filey

Primrose Valley has changed almost out of recognition since pre-war days; it is now one of the biggest holiday complexes in England. However, this early 1930s view is how some still like to remember it.

Chapter Four:
FISHING AND THE LIFEBOAT SERVICE

Fishing

We know from ecclesiastical records that as long ago as the Twelfth Century men were fishing from Filey and landing their catches as far away as Whitby and Grimsby. It is also perhaps surprising that in the early Nineteenth Century, Filey and Staithes were the two most important fishing stations on the Yorkshire coast. In Victorian times between two and three hundred Filey men earned their living catching fish; although the number actively engaged in fishing today is now very much less, it is still of major importance to Filey's economy.

This remarkable group consists of about half the total strength of Filey fishermen in the mid-1880s.
The occasion was the presentation of new oil-skins and sou'westers by a prospective member of parliament for Buckrose, the constituency in which Filey was then situated. It is not known if his generosity was followed by his election!

Scarborough Harbour was the home port for the Filey yawl fleet which in late Victorian times numbered over 30. Taking a break at the turn of the century while working on the yawl *Lucy* are, standing at the back, Jack Crimlis and Frank Baxter. Seated are Mark Jenkinson, his son John William, Mark's brother Dick who was the skipper and Will. C. Cammish spending a day on board during his school holidays. In later life Will. had a fine singing voice and became widely known as the Yorkshire Baritone.

Jack Crimlis was drowned in the Red Sea trying to save a shipmate while serving in the Royal Navy.

An added interest to this study of three local stalwarts is the indication it gives of the sturdy nature of the carriages used for carrying cobles. Are the clay pipes, apparently being smoked by the two gentlemen seated, the 'real thing' or have they been added later by the photographer?

In local fishing, girls and women had a vital part to play. Many would frequently walk several miles to shore-lines
where limpets and mussels could be found. These they would prise from the rock, carry them back to Filey
and use them to bait fishing-lines.

Illustrated here is Mrs. Alf. Powley dressed as she would be when prepared for a day gathering flithers
(the local name for limpets).

Shown also is Susannah Johnson (née Cappleman) in 1896 at the age of 11 years. Heavy loads were often carried on the head
using a sand-filled stocking as a circular support. Mrs. Johnson lived to be, at 104 years-of-age, Filey's oldest-ever resident.

What a wealth of experience is shared by these five fishermen, now retired from the sea. No doubt as they met together at the Cliff-Top they would reminisce about the storms they survived, the nights spent baiting lines for cod on the Dogger Bank and weeks away from home following the herring down the coast as far as Great Yarmouth.

A fisherman's interest in his former calling seldom ceases on retirement. If he is not on the Coble Landing to see the boats return he can probably be found on the cliff top at the end of Queen Street. This is still a splendid vantage point for the Brigg, the Bay and the Beach.

Here, about 1910, Messrs. Cammish, Mark Jenkinson, Tom Crimlisk, Frank Baxter, Simpson, George Colling and Bill Jenkinson reminisce while missing little of what is happening in the Bay.

Pausing briefly at mid-day for the photographer, following a fishing-trip which would have begun in the early hours, are William 'Cobby' Hunter and Matthew Colling. Frank Wheeler is giving a hand in getting the lines back up to the town where they would be cleaned and baited ready for the next trip to sea. The last task of the day would be removing the leather sea-boots; not an easy one, especially when wet.

In the early part of the Century sailing-ships of all types were being replaced by powered vessels. The yawls in which many Filey men spent their fishing careers had all gone by the end of World War One. The yawls were generally succeeded by drifters and trawlers and generations of Filey fishermen owned and sailed in both. Yawls would sometimes beach in Filey Bay to load and unload but this was impossible with powered vessels and Scarborough Harbour continued to be the home port for Filey men. The drifter *Rose Duncan*, owned by George Scotter and William Sayers, is shown leaving the harbour at Scarborough for the fishing grounds in the early 1930s.

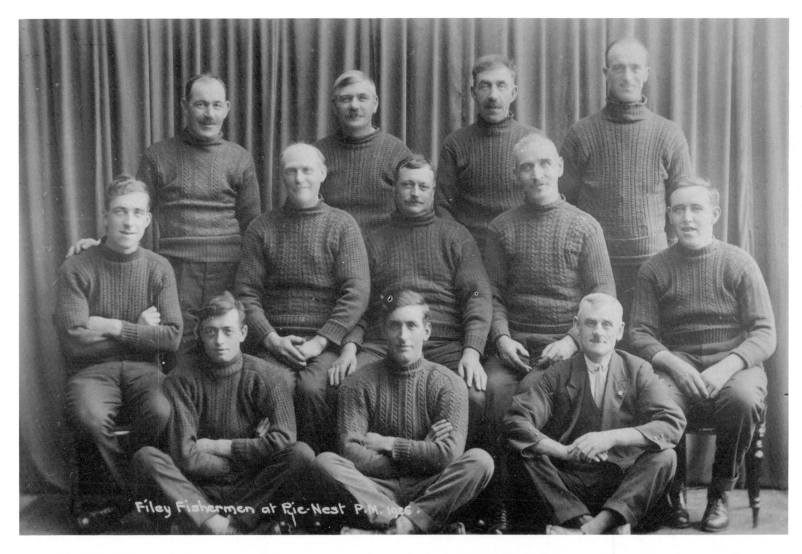

Filey Fishermen at Pie-Nest P.M. 1926.

The Filey Fishermen's Choir has its origins over a hundred years ago in the bands of local fishermen who would walk many miles on a Sunday to lead services in Methodist Chapels. The present Choir members still take many services of song each year, sometimes going as far afield as their predecessors shown here at Pie-Nest Primitive Methodist Chapel, Halifax in 1926.
The members are, from left to right:
Matt. Haxby (Senior), Jimmy Douglas, Richard Willis, Tom (Tich) Jenkinson,
middle row: Tom Willis, William (Billie Calam) Cammish, Edward Scales Jenkinson (Senior), Tom Crimlisk (Senior), Tom Crimlisk (Junior).
front row: Edward Scales Jenkinson (Junior), Frank Hanson, E. Jenkinson.

The skilful co-operation of men and horses in launching and recovering cobles never ceased to fascinate and impress visitors to Filey. In this photograph taken soon after World War Two, Duke, Bob and Bonny are performing a task they had carried out many times before. The rider is George Appleby whose horses they were.
The three men whose necessary job it was to assist in getting the cobles on to and off their carriages, often in darkness and rough seas, are Mark Henry Scotter, John William 'Lorty' Jenkinson and Thomas 'Hopper' Johnson. Mr. Jenkinson lost his arm in a brick-yard accident; in the Season he was an able sand-artist on Bridlington Beach.

A familiar sight in 1930s Filey was the crab and lobster stall of Mr. and Mrs. James 'Bass' Wyvill.

5720 Fisherfolk Mending Nets at Filey.

Fishing nets are easily damaged in use and mending them is less of a chore if it can be done with friends. This relaxed group, clearly enjoying the sunshine, is working at the top of Church Hill.

It is perhaps surprising that Filey has been an important fishing station for many centuries even though it has never had a harbour. Here, in addition to the difficulties associated with the actual job of catching fish is the arduous task of launching the boats and bringing them back on shore. As is clearly shown here, even with the aid of a tractor, moving a coble on land could require the efforts of several men working together. In addition to the tractor-driver there are at least eight fishermen and launchers straining to get the coble correctly placed on its carriage. the coble is the *Edward and Muriel*, the driver is Bill Simpson and the fisherman nearest to the tractor is Thomas 'Boysher' Cappleman who was the Lifeboat Coxwain from 1935 to 1947. The year is probably 1946.

In the 1940s tractors replaced horses for launching and recovering cobles. These operations were thus made somewhat easier to carry out mainly because a tractor can push as well as pull. However, considerable skill is still required by both driver and launchers as this picture illustrates. The tractor exhausts are vertical for obvious reasons; the other unusual feature is the driver's vertical protective board.
The coble is *Windsor Lad II*, built in 1949 by John Burrell; the crew members are William 'Dag' Chapman, William Robinson and his son Charles.

The Filey Life-boat

The Filey Life-boat Station was established in 1823 although it was then a local undertaking until it was adopted by the R.N.L.I. about thirty years later. As the service-boards in the Life-boat House indicate, many dramatic rescues were performed by the succession of boats stationed here and scores of seamen and fishermen have been saved from certain death as a result of stress of storm.

Until 1940 the life-boats relied on sail and oar for their motive power; however, the crew-members now have at their disposal a fast, modern and well equipped Mersey class boat together with an inshore rescue boat which has proved invaluable for emergencies close to the shore-line.

This interesting study shows the life-boat in its house with two old stalwarts, John Crimlisk and Frankie Baxter.

This studio photograph of James Wheeler shows how cumbersome to wear must have been the cork life-jackets which were standard issue for many years.

Lifeboat naming ceremonies are always important and memorable occasions. The boat shown here is *Hollon The Third* on 4th May 1907; built at a cost of £955 it remained on station here for thirty years during which it carried out many remarkable rescue operations.

For many years it was a tradition of Lifeboat Day that the boat was drawn by horses around the town. The difficulty of manoeuvring, with six horses, the boat on its carriage through Filey's streets is well illustrated here. Preceded by Filey Silver Band the lifeboat negotiates a corner before proceeding up Southdene. The year is about 1912.

This evocative study of horses and boat on Lifeboat Day 1930 again features *Hollon III*.

For obvious reasons, photographs of the lifeboat at night are rare; this one shows *The Isa and Penrhyn Milstead* returning from service about 1960.

Standing near the bow are Stan. 'Trab' Cammish and Matt. 'Sailor' Jenkinson; near the stern is Thomas 'Snosh' Jenkinson who was Chairman of Filey Urban District Council during the years 1966-1967 and 1970-1971.

The Filey Life-Saving Rocket Brigade Company has many fine rescues to its credit. Vessels would sometimes be driven ashore in local waters in places where the lifeboat was unable to reach them. Frequently, on such occasions, the Company has been able to fire a line across a vessel, thus enabling a breeches buoy apparatus to be secured and sailors in imminent danger to be hauled safely ashore.

The Company is seen here on practice night about 1960.

In July 1955, HRH The Princess Royal came to Filey formally to open The Royal Parade. Additional events in the day were an inspection of the lifeboat crew and the presentation of the B.E.M. to Thomas 'Titch' Jenkinson for services to the fishing industry. The day was fine and warm and all events were much enjoyed by residents and visitors.

Chapter Five:

PEOPLE: OCCASIONS: EARLY FLYING DAYS AND BUTLIN'S HOLIDAY CAMP

People

The character of a town depends very much on its built environment and on the people who make a permanent or even transient contribution to its welfare.

The photographs which follow show just a very few of those who, through the years, have been a part of Filey's day-to-day life.

The numerical strength of the staff of Filey Station about 1900, then part of the North Eastern Railway, confirms how very important to Filey was the system when most journeys to or from the town were made by rail and the goods depôt (where is now Silver Birches) dealt with most of the items of commerce which were moved in or out of the town.

The rapid development of the internal combustion engine in the early years of the century is confirmed by this splendid study of an immaculate member of Mr. Harry Smart's fleet of vehicles in 1914.

In the background can be seen the entrance to the then Ravine Hall estate.

The place where Mr. Hall of Muston stands with his daughters to have his photograph taken has now a very different aspect for it is part of the Station Avenue roundabout. The baskets on the cart would seem to indicate that the Hall family are in the middle of their weekly egg-round.

In the days prior to the introduction of a local authority cleansing service, disposal of domestic refuse was often by deposition on the Beach or in Church Ravine. The Council dustcart was therefore a major asset in the campaign to keep Filey clean. In 1920 the team manning the solid-tyred vehicle comprised Bob. Watkinson, Bill Scales and Jack Jenkinson.
The location is outside Matt. Haxby's grocer's shop at the corner of Scarborough Road and West Parade (now West Road).

Photographs of Filey in either World War One or Two are few in number; this is mainly because film was almost impossible to obtain and also because Filey was in a security-conscious zone and anyone observed with a camera could be arrested on suspicion of being a spy.

This informal view of members of the Royal Horse Artillery cleaning horse-harness well conveys the atmosphere of Filey in war-time. The location is that of Belle Vue Crescent and Station Avenue car-park and the time is about 1916.

During both Wars Filey was a garrison town with hotels and boarding-houses being commandeered for service use. In the first conflict the Border Regiment and the Hunts. Cyclists Regiment were amongst those which had troops stationed here; in the second, many members of the Free French Air-Force trained in Filey.

In the days before local radio and daily newspapers the bellman, or town-crier, fulfilled a most important function. This studio portrait is of Tom Webb who was Filey's bellman for many years. He would announce coming events, articles lost and found and also on occasions, for a consideration, arrange with discretion, meetings between young ladies and gentlemen who might wish to meet but who had not been formally introduced.

A remarkable man by any standards, the Reverend Arthur Neville Cooper was Vicar of Filey from 1880 to 1935. A conscientious pastor to his people who was both liked and respected he was also exceptional in the very long walks he undertook in his annual holidays in the middle years of his ministry. His first long walk was to London which, having left Filey after Evensong one Sunday he reached London in time to return by train for morning service the following Sunday. In later years he walked several times across Europe reaching on foot, amongst other places, Rome, Monte Carlo, Budapest, Barcelona and Vienna. His very readable accounts of his walks can still occasionally be found in second-hand book-shops.

Local Government in Filey has been the responsibility of several bodies. In 1855 the aptly-named Nuisance Removal Committee was formed; this was succeeded in 1868 by the Local Board of Health. In January 1895 the Filey Urban District Council was created with much greater powers for administering Filey's affairs. Under re-organisation in 1974, many of these powers passed to Scarborough Borough Council but the newly-formed Filey Town Council continued as the body 'closest to the people'. Shown here, in 1955, are members and officials of F.U.D.C.; they are from the left;

back row: Alan Kelly (Surveyor), George Barker, Ken. Martin (Entertainments), Mrs. D. M. Cousins, Jack Cunningham, Mrs. M. R. Marriot, George Doran, Ken. Henderson (Clerk), K. Skeats (Housing).

front row: Ken. Dowson, David Watkins, Leonard Hallam, Frank Scaife, Frank Welbourn, Maurice Medcalf, Edwin Corrigan.

In early post-World War II days, a visit to the Southdene Pavilion for an evening's Concert Party entertainment was one of the highlights of a summer holiday in Filey.
In the 1950s a popular producer was Billy Scott-Comber (The Smiling Irishman). In this group photograph he is wearing a 'topper'. This party included all the essential artists; dancers, singers (including a young soubrette), comedian and magician.
For several seasons a concert-party and a repertory company were engaged jointly by Butlin's Ltd. and Filey Urban District Council; they each performed 3 days every week in both places.
In days before universal access to television, full-houses were frequent at the Pavilion.

Comic football matches on the Beach between teams of fishermen and firemen were popular occasions in the 1950s. This group of elegantly attired gentlemen represented the firemen in what was clearly a very well supported game.
From left to right the players are: George Burton, Bob. Garrett, Ivor Roberts, Arthur Haxby, Jack Jenkinson, George Harris, Cliff. Pashby, Alf. Gray, -----, -----, Tommy Simpson.

Occasions

Special occasions are highlights in all our lives and are much valued in their recollection. The following are some which their participants would no doubt remember with much happiness. Those illustrated include an excursion, a friendly society's day by the sea, a street party and, that most memorable of all occasions, a wedding.

Few photographs survive of early scenes at the Railway Station. This one was taken on 12th June 1905 and shows one of several trains arranged to bring spectators to the Motor Speed Trials on the beach. The locomotive is North Eastern Railway number 675. Locomotives of this type continued in operation on the Scarborough to Hull line until after World War Two.

This splendid group of undoubtedly upright citizens is the Filey Town's Committee, formed to organise a major local event. This was the day-trip to Filey on 4th May 1907 of the Yorkshire Fire Brigades Friendly Society. The location for the photograph is the Crescent Gardens. Only one member of the group can be identified; William Gofton, councillor, auctioneer and valuer is half-kneeling on the grass; respected and well-liked, he was a friend of the author's family.

How fortunate that it was a calm day when this Edwardian wedding group assembled, otherwise some difficulty would, no doubt, have been experienced with the fine array of hats.

The wedding ceremony was probably conducted at Ebenezer Methodist Chapel as the place arranged for the photograph, the C. of E. Infants' School playground, is just across the road. Sledmere Court now stands on the site.

Why was it that the women guests considerably outnumbered the men? Perhaps it was because the men were unable to take time off work.

It is clear that the Brook Bond Tea, three-cornered hats were not an outstanding success at this 1953 Queen Street Coronation Day party.

How fortunate it is that someone with a good camera was on hand to capture, on film, the spirit of this joyful event. An added bonus is that he (or she) chose the fishermen's cottages as a background; good photographs of these much-missed homes are rare indeed.

Early Flying Days

For just two years from 1910 to 1912 Filey Beach was an important location in the development of flying. The beach proved to be ideal as a ready-made surface for taking-off and landing and at the Filey Flying School, several pilots learned to fly. It was also an early testing-ground for The Blackburn Aircraft Company. A hangar, and a bungalow for the staff, were built on the cliff between Primrose Valley and Hunmanby Gap; part of the slipway leading from the hangar to the beach remains. Aircraft were brought to Filey by rail and shown here is part of the fuselage of a Bleriot 25 h.p. monoplane arriving at Filey Station in 1910.

This photograph shows the Bleriot partly assembled. The pilot is almost certainly Bentfield C. Hucks who taught himself to fly at Filey and is credited with being the first Englishman to perform the manoeuvre known as looping-the-loop.

The pilot's pride in the fully assembled Bleriot is evident as he stands at the top of the slipway with the aviators'
bungalow in the background.
The tail wheel appears to have been replaced by shaped metal tubing.

Ready to take to the air and perhaps only waiting for the tide to go out is this Blackburn Mercury in 1911 poised at the top of the slipway.
Comparison with the Bleriot of 1910 indicates how rapidly aircraft development was taking place.
The method for supporting the wings is clearly shown as is the steering wheel for controlling the tail fin.

On 12th July 1960 a display was arranged by the Blackburn Aircraft Company to commemorate the golden jubilee of flying at Filey.
Part of the full afternoon's programme was a series of manoeuvres performed by pilot Derek Whitehead in the 1932 Blackburn B.2 Trainer shown here.
(By courtesy of British Aerospace, Brough).

Butlin's Holiday Camp

The story of Butlin's at Filey is an interesting one. Building had just begun in 1939 when World War Two broke out; however, construction work continued so that the Camp could be used for military purposes. The R.A.F. Regiment spent some of its earliest days stationed there during which period the base was designated as R.A.F. Hunmanby Moor.
In 1945 conversion to a Holiday Camp took place rapidly and the parade-ground became the boating-lake. In peace-time years the Camp continued to grow in size and importance until it became one of the largest holiday centres in the World.

This splendid view of Butlin's in 1967 at the peak of its popularity will no doubt evoke many happy memories in the minds of those who stayed at or visited the Camp. Accommodating up to 10,000 visitors who would be looked after by 1,500 staff it played a vital part in Filey's economy until it closed in 1984.
The complex of facilities grouped around the lake includes (taken in a clockwise direction) dining-hall, Regency Ballroom, coffee bar, theatre, shops, indoor and outdoor swimming pools, theatre, French Bar, Viennese Ballroom and dining hall.

The Regency Ballroom at Butlin's Camp was certainly one of the most splendid in the North of England. This postcard well portrays the ornate decoration which contributed to the atmosphere created by a crowded dance-floor at the height of the Season. Particularly memorable of the events held here were the Dance Festivals; they were major occasions in Britain's Dance Calendar.

POSTSCRIPT

The various aspects of Filey in its natural setting have provided popular subjects for professional and amateur photographers and artists for almost one and a half centuries and we are fortunate to have available to us so many images of Victorian, Edwardian and later Filey.

From them we can deduce something of the vision shared by earlier Filonians as they sought to create a built environment worthy of its location. Today, Filey's residents and regular visitors are equally determined to ensure that the town and surroundings we have inherited shall be cared for, and even cherished, for our own enjoyment and that of future generations.